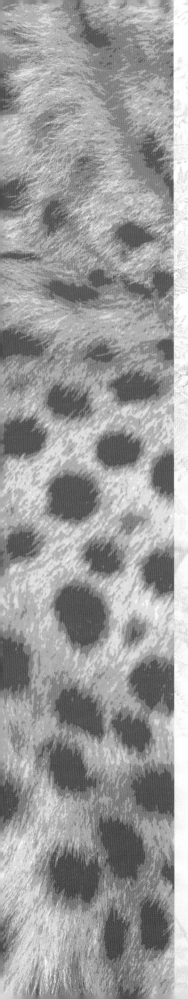

Contents

KU-032-561

Any words appearing in the text in bold, **like this**, are explained in the Glossary.

Introducing mammals

Mammals are found almost everywhere in the world, from the tropical rainforests to the frozen poles, on land, in the air and in water. There are more than 4600 different types of mammal. They are the only animals that have hair and feed their young on milk.

Mammals belong to a large group of animals called **vertebrates**. These are animals with backbones. The backbone is made up of small bones hinged together, with a group of nerves (the spinal cord) running through the middle. Other vertebrates include fish, amphibians, reptiles and birds.

Teeth, ears and hair

Adult mammals usually have four types of teeth: incisors, **canines**, premolars and molars. The teeth are **adapted** to suit the diet of the mammal. They also usually have an outer ear, or pinna, on the outside of their heads to funnel sounds into the inner ear.

Only mammals have true hair, which grows continuously from the root. Hair is made of a substance called keratin. Hair can be thick, forming fur, or sparse as it is on the human body.

Whiskers, spines and some horns are made of **modified** hair. Some mammals, such as hippos and whales, have lost their hair as an adaptation to their environment.

Classification key

KINGDOM	Animalia
PHYLUM	Chordata
SUB-PHYLUM	Vertebrata
CLASS	**Mammalia**

▶ Brown bears have thick fur to trap heat and keep them warm.

www.raintreepublishers.co.uk

Visit our website to find out more information about **Raintree** books.

To order:

 Phone 44 (0) 1865 888113

Send a fax to 44 (0) 1865 314091

Visit the Raintree Bookshop at **www.raintreepublishers.co.uk** to browse our catalogue and order online.

Produced for Raintree by
White-Thomson Publishing Ltd
Bridgewater Business Centre, 210 High Street,
Lewes, East Sussex, BN7 2NH

First published in Great Britain by Raintree, Halley Court, Jordan Hill, Oxford, OX2 8EJ, part of Harcourt Education.
Raintree is a registered trademark of Harcourt Education Ltd.

Consultant: Dr Rod Preston-Mafham
Editorial: Katie Orchard, Nick Hunter and Catherine Clarke
Design: Tim Mayer
Picture Research: Sally Morgan
Production: Jonathan Smith

Originated by Dot Gradations Ltd
Printed in China by WKT Company Limited

ISBN 1 844 43766 3 (hardback) ISBN 1 844 43776 0 (paperback)
09 08 07 06 05   10 09 08 07 06
10 9 8 7 6 5 4 3 2 1   10 9 8 7 6 5 4 3 2 1

British Library Cataloguing in Publication Data
Morgan, Sally
Mammals – (Animal Kingdom)
599
A full catalogue record for this book is available from the British Library

Acknowledgements
The publishers would like to thank the following for permission to reproduce photographs: Corbis **Title page**, **60** bottom; Digital Stock pp.**10**, **16**, **33** top, **38**; Digital Vision pp.**4**, **8**, **13** top, **15** top left, **29** bottom, **31** top, **35**, **51**, **58**, **60** top; Ecoscene pp.**9** bottom (Fritz Pölking), **11** top (Christine Osborne), **17** top (Fritz Pölking), **19** (Brandon Cole / V&W), **24** top (Fritz Pölking), **26** top and **27** top (S. Tiwari), **28** (Karl Ammann), **30** (Fritz Pölking), **39** top (Robin Redfern), **42** (Philip Colla), **43** top and bottom, and **44** bottom left (Brandon Cole / V&W), **44** main, **45**, and **46** (Philip Colla), **47** bottom (Brandon Cole / V&W), **49** middle (Michael Gore), **55** top (Robert Baldwin), **55** bottom (Tom Ennis), **56** (Pete Cairns), **57** top (Fritz Pölking), **59** (Philip Colla); Ecoscene – Papilio pp.**13** bottom (Dennis Johnson), **48** bottom and **49** top (Robert Pickett); Nature Picture Library pp.**9** top (George McCarthy), **15** bottom and **21** bottom (Anup Shah), **24** bottom (Bruce Davidson), **25** main (Brian Lightfoot), **26** main (Anup Shah), **31** bottom (Bruce Davidson), **34** top (T.J. Rich), **36** (Richard Du Toit), **39** bottom (Peter Blackwell), **47** top (Aflo), **50** left (Ingo Arndt), **57** bottom (Staffan Widstrand); NHPA pp.**5** bottom right (Martin Harvey), **6** and **7** (Jonathan and Angela Scott), **7** top (Laurie Campbell), **7** bottom (Martin Harvey), **11** bottom (Joe Blossom), **12** (Martin Harvey), **14** (ANT), **17** bottom (Christophe Ratier), **18** top (Kevin Schafer), **18** bottom (Nick Garbutt), **20** (Mike Lane), **21** top (Jonathan and Angela Scott), **22–23** and **23** bottom (Nigel Dennis), **23** top (G.I. Bernard), **29** top (Martin Harvey), **32** top (Laurie Campbell), **32** bottom (Daryl Balfour), **34** bottom (Martin Harvey), **37** top right (Anthony Bannister), **40** top (Daniel Heuclin), **40** bottom (Guy Edwardes), **41** (Michael Leach), **50** right and **52** top (ANT), **52** bottom (Daniel Heuclin), **53** (Dave Watts), **54–55** (T. Kitchen and V. Hirst); Photodisc pp. **5** top right, **37** bottom left.

Cover photograph of zebra reproduced with permission of NHPA (Kevin Schafer).

Every effort has been made to contact copyright holders of any material reproduced in this book.
Any omissions will be rectified in subsequent printings if notice is given to the publishers.
The paper used to print this book comes from sustainable resources.

Adaptable animals

Mammals are highly adaptable, and are able to change their behaviour to suit their environment. One feature that makes mammals adaptable is their ability to maintain a constant body temperature, regardless of the temperature of their surroundings. This is called **endothermy**. For example, a polar bear's thick fur and layer of fat trap heat so it can keep its body temperature at around 37° Celsius, even when the outside temperature may be well below freezing. Mammals are not the only endothermic animals – birds can regulate their body temperature, too. Other animals, such as reptiles, have a body temperature that changes with their surroundings and they become inactive at low temperatures.

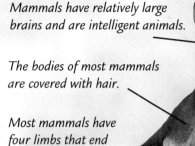

The outer ear funnels sound into the inner ear, which is within the skull.

Mammals have relatively large brains and are intelligent animals.

The bodies of most mammals are covered with hair.

Most mammals have four limbs that end in **digits**.

▶ Mammals share many similar **characteristics**.

◀ Female mammals feed their young with milk from special glands, called **mammary glands**. It is from these glands that mammals get their name.

Classification

Living **organisms** are classified, or organized, according to how closely related one organism is to another. A **species** is a group of individuals that are similar to each other and that can **interbreed** with one another. Species are grouped together into genera. A single genus may contain a number of species that share some features. Genera are grouped together in families, the families grouped into orders and the orders grouped into classes. Mammals belong to the class Mammalia. Classes are grouped together in phyla (singular phylum) and finally the phyla are grouped into kingdoms. Kingdoms are the largest groups. Mammals belong to the animal kingdom. (To find out more see pages 58–59.)

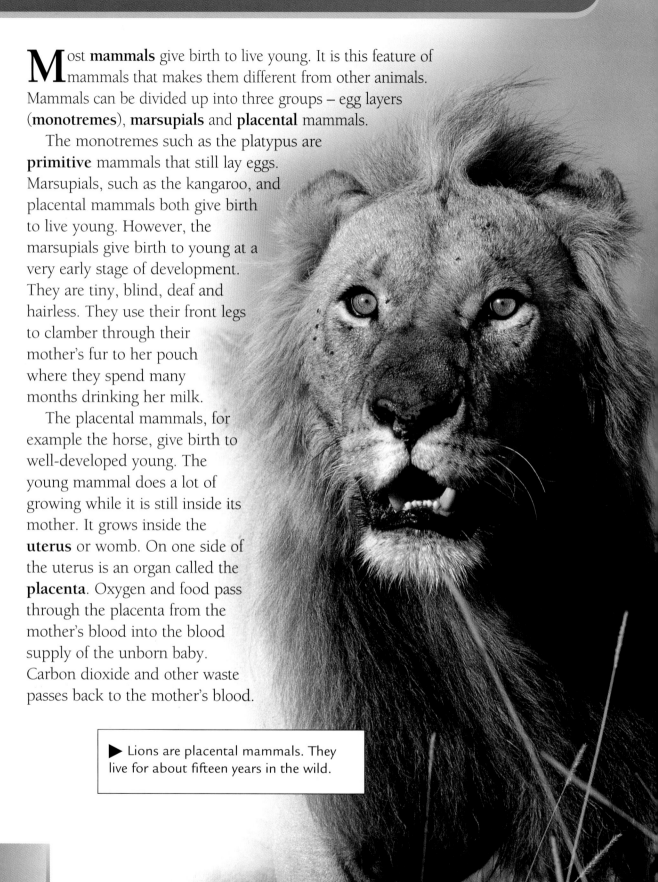

Most **mammals** give birth to live young. It is this feature of mammals that makes them different from other animals. Mammals can be divided up into three groups – egg layers (**monotremes**), **marsupials** and **placental** mammals.

The monotremes such as the platypus are **primitive** mammals that still lay eggs. Marsupials, such as the kangaroo, and placental mammals both give birth to live young. However, the marsupials give birth to young at a very early stage of development. They are tiny, blind, deaf and hairless. They use their front legs to clamber through their mother's fur to her pouch where they spend many months drinking her milk.

The placental mammals, for example the horse, give birth to well-developed young. The young mammal does a lot of growing while it is still inside its mother. It grows inside the **uterus** or womb. On one side of the uterus is an organ called the **placenta**. Oxygen and food pass through the placenta from the mother's blood into the blood supply of the unborn baby. Carbon dioxide and other waste passes back to the mother's blood.

▶ Lions are placental mammals. They live for about fifteen years in the wild.

The length of time between the **fertilization** of the egg and birth is called the **gestation period**. In small mammals such as mice and rats, the gestation period is just a few weeks. The babies are born hairless and helpless. Gestation is much longer in larger mammals: for example the gestation period of the human is nine months.

▲ This guanaco is giving birth to her young. The new-born guanaco will be able to run around within minutes of birth.

Parental care

Female mammals feed their babies milk produced by their **mammary glands**. The milk contains all the nutrition the baby needs. The babies are fed milk until their teeth develop and they can chew adult food. The change from milk to solid food is called weaning. Some mammals look after their young for years. Other mammals produce young that can live independently within a few weeks.

Life span

In general, the larger the mammal, the longer its life span. The longest-lived mammals include humans, elephants and whales. Some of the smallest mammals, such as shrews, have very short life spans. They grow quickly, have a very fast heartbeat and live for only a year or two.

▼ Mammals such as this ring-tailed lemur care for their young until they are able to look after themselves.

Amazing facts

- The female lemming gives birth sixteen days after **mating** and can produce up to twelve babies. Each baby is ready to mate at three weeks!

- The male brown antechinus (a marsupial) lives for just a few months. He only fathers one litter, but does not live long enough to see the birth of his offspring.

7

Staying warm

Imagine living in a place where the temperatures can fall to -45° Celsius. Amazingly, some **mammals** such as the polar bear and the Arctic fox can survive these temperatures. Mammals can keep their body temperature almost constant, even though the temperature of their surroundings may change. They have various ways of keeping their temperature within a narrow range. If their body temperature falls, mammals may shiver or raise their hairs to trap heat. They move around to generate heat. If the temperature rises, mammals lose heat by sweating or panting. However, for mammals that live in permanently cold climates these simple methods are not enough. Their bodies have **adapted**, or changed, to cope with the climate.

Fur and fat

Polar mammals have to eat lots of food in order to produce enough heat to keep warm. They cannot afford to lose body heat, so good **insulation** is essential. Their bodies are covered in thick fur and they have a layer of **blubber** (fat) under their skin. Blubber is so good at trapping heat that the skin above it may feel cold to the touch but the mammal is perfectly warm inside.

▲ Sea lions have a thick layer of blubber and waterproof fur.

This dormouse looks as if it is asleep, but it is actually hibernating.

Hibernation

Many small mammals such as dormice, hedgehogs and bats **hibernate**, or go into a deep sleep, during the winter. Their small size and large surface area means they have to eat a lot of food each day just to keep warm. Food can be in short supply during winter so they survive by hibernating. During the autumn they build up layers of fat and then creep into a nest and sleep. Their heart beats very slowly and their body temperature falls to just above that of their surroundings. They survive by using up their fat reserves. Their bodies just 'tick over' until the outside temperatures rise again and more food becomes available.

Amazing facts

- The Arctic fox is so well insulated that it can sleep on the snow at temperatures of –80° Celsius for up to 1 hour without coming to any harm.

- A polar bear can easily overheat if it runs too fast! It may eat snow or lie flat on the ice to cool off.

▼ A polar bear may look white, but underneath the fur its skin is black. Dark skin absorbs more heat than light skin.

Surviving in the desert

Desert **mammals** have **adapted** to survive extremes of temperature. Daytime temperatures can soar to 50° Celsius. If a mammal's body temperature rises by just a few degrees, it may die from heat stroke. At night, the desert can be very cold so the mammal then has to keep warm.

Keeping cool

To cool down, mammals start to sweat or pant. Sweat **glands** in the skin produce a watery liquid, which **evaporates**, cooling the skin. Not all mammals sweat. Dogs, for example, cool off by panting. They open their mouths and hang out their tongues to increase the surface area from which water can evaporate. Many mammals avoid lying in the hot sun. They move into the shade or crawl into underground burrows, only coming out at night when it is cooler.

A few mammals can actually trick their brain into thinking that their body temperature is cooler than it really is. Normally, the cooling processes start to work when the body reaches a certain temperature. The desert oryx cools its blood as it flows through the nose. This cooled blood goes to the brain and the brain thinks the temperature is acceptable. This means that valuable water is not lost in sweating and panting.

◄ A desert oryx can walk for hours to find food. During the hottest hours of the day they rest under the shade of the trees.

▲ A camel's hump is full of fat, which can be used when there is no food around.

Amazing camel facts

- Camels have long eyelashes and slit-like nostrils that can close during sand storms.
- Their thick fur **insulates** against the heat during the day and prevents heat loss at night.
- Adult camels can drink as much as 136 litres of water within a very short period of time.

Finding water

Desert mammals have to be able to find enough water to survive. Many rely on the water contained in the plants that they eat. They eat fleshy fruits and leaves full of water. Some mammals can get enough water from eating seeds and never drink water at all.

Body shape

Desert mammals tend to have a body shape that helps to lose heat rather than conserve it. For example, they are often slim, long-legged animals. This creates a large surface area over which heat can be lost. Blood flows close to the surface of the skin to lose heat. Some large mammals live in hot climates, for example elephants, rhinos and hippos. They have difficulty in cooling off because the centre of their body is a long way from the surface. They do not have hair so heat can escape more easily from the surface of their skin. Elephants have large ears and can keep cool by flapping them.

▶ Fennec foxes hunt at night when it is cooler. Their long ears enable them to hear their **prey** moving around over the desert in the dark.

Feeding

▼ Aye-ayes use their long claw to pull out larvae from trees.

Mammals feed in many different ways. A mammal's diet depends on the shape of its jaw and the arrangement of its teeth. Adult mammals have four different kinds of teeth: incisors, **canines**, premolars and molars.

Carnivores, or meat eaters, have long, curved canines for stabbing and killing their **prey**, while rodents have large incisors for gnawing. **Herbivores**, or plant eaters, have large, ridged molars, which are ideal for grinding plant food.

Termite eaters

Each day, giant anteaters, armadillos and pangolins feed on thousands of ants and termites. Their claws are long and curved (ideal for ripping open termite nests) and they have a long tongue, covered in gluey **saliva** so that the termites stick to it.

The bodies of armadillos and pangolins are covered in tough scales, which act like a coat of armour. When hundreds of angry termites swarm out to protect their nest, these mammals simply press their scales firmly together, close their eyelids and nostrils and keep on eating!

Amazing facts

- The aye-aye, a type of lemur, has an incredibly long, thin middle finger that ends in a claw. It uses this finger to pull out **larvae** from inside holes in trees.
- The vampire bat feeds on blood from other mammals. It carefully shaves the hair from a patch of skin using its incisor teeth and then uses its canine teeth to cut two grooves, lapping up the blood, which oozes from the cut.
- The giant armadillo is the mammal with the most teeth – it has about 100!

◀ Chimps have hands that can grip food, or tools such as this twig – handy for reaching termites!

Tool users

Chimpanzees have hands similar to humans, with a thumb that lies at a right angle to the fingers. This means that they can grip and **manipulate** objects. Chimpanzees have learnt to use tools to help them find food. The chimp, for example, will poke a stick into a termites' nest. The termites grip on to the stick and then the chimp pulls the stick out and licks off the termites.

Herbivores

The savannah grasslands of southern Africa are home to many different types of herbivores. Many feed on grass, but others eat the leaves of the trees and shrubs. Although there are large numbers of herbivores they do not always compete with each other for food. For example, several different types of herbivores feed on the leaves of the acacia tree. Small antelope and impala eat leaves from the lower branches while the gerenuk stands on its back legs to reach the higher leaves. The giraffe, tallest of all the mammals, **browses** on leaves near the top of the tree.

▶ An extra-long neck allows these giraffes to reach the higher leaves that other animals cannot reach.

Mammal movement

Walking, running, jumping, flying and swimming – all these types of movement can be found among the **mammals**. Most mammals have four limbs, but in some the limbs have **adapted** for a particular type of movement.

Hoofs for running

Hoofed mammals such as zebra and antelope have long legs for running over great distances. The longer the legs, the quicker they can run. They have to be able to outrun their **predators**. These predators have adapted to be able to run fast over short distances, and are equipped with powerful muscles.

Flight

Only three groups of animals can fly: birds, insects and bats. Bats are mammals. Bats have arms that form a wing for flying. The wing is like a thin sheet formed from a double layer of skin. It stretches from the legs and the side of the body to the fingers. They have four long fingers to support the wing.

▼ Bats are nocturnal and fly at night. This Australian ghost bat has a wingspan of about 50 centimetres. It hunts large insects, reptiles, frogs, birds and small mammals.

The gibbon moves with ease through the trees, swinging from branch to branch. This method of movement is called brachiation.

Amazing facts

- The largest European bat is the large mouse-eared bat, which has a wingspan of up to 38 centimetres. It travels 200 kilometres (125 miles) across Europe between its winter and summer feeding places.

- The colugo, or flying lemur, can glide over distances of up to 136 metres. It has a huge **membrane** stretched between its arms, legs and head to form a 'wing'. However, the colugo's wing is so large that it can hardly move on the ground.

- Male western grey kangaroos can travel more than 10 metres in a single leap.

Swinging through trees

Mammals that live in trees tend to have long limbs, which they use to climb and swing through the branches. Gibbons, a type of ape, live their entire lives in the trees. They have very long arms, which are ideal for swinging from branch to branch, and no tail. They can move at great speed through the trees and have been described as the acrobats of the mammal world.

Swimming

Marine mammals such as whales, dolphins and seals live in water and their bodies are adapted to swimming. These mammals have a **streamlined** shape that tapers to the tail. When moving through water it is important to have a smooth outline to slip through the water easily. Whales and dolphins do not have any hairs on their skin and this creates an even smoother surface. Marine mammals use flippers – limbs that are rounded and paddle-like – to steer. The whale has a huge tail fin, which pushes the animal through the water.

The hoofed feet of the warthog allow it to move quickly over hard ground.

15

The cheetah

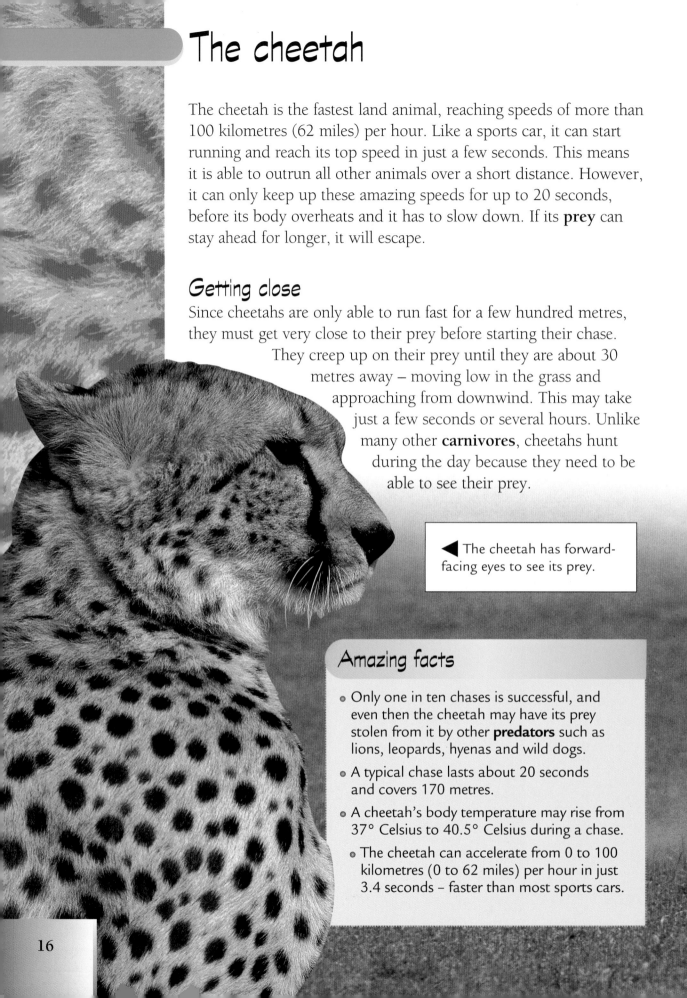

The cheetah is the fastest land animal, reaching speeds of more than 100 kilometres (62 miles) per hour. Like a sports car, it can start running and reach its top speed in just a few seconds. This means it is able to outrun all other animals over a short distance. However, it can only keep up these amazing speeds for up to 20 seconds, before its body overheats and it has to slow down. If its **prey** can stay ahead for longer, it will escape.

Getting close

Since cheetahs are only able to run fast for a few hundred metres, they must get very close to their prey before starting their chase. They creep up on their prey until they are about 30 metres away – moving low in the grass and approaching from downwind. This may take just a few seconds or several hours. Unlike many other **carnivores**, cheetahs hunt during the day because they need to be able to see their prey.

◀ The cheetah has forward-facing eyes to see its prey.

Amazing facts

- Only one in ten chases is successful, and even then the cheetah may have its prey stolen from it by other **predators** such as lions, leopards, hyenas and wild dogs.
- A typical chase lasts about 20 seconds and covers 170 metres.
- A cheetah's body temperature may rise from 37° Celsius to 40.5° Celsius during a chase.
- The cheetah can accelerate from 0 to 100 kilometres (0 to 62 miles) per hour in just 3.4 seconds – faster than most sports cars.

The chase

The cheetah gets its speed from its extremely flexible **skeleton**, which allows its backbone to curve up and down to give a long stride. The cheetah may be able to run very fast in a straight line, but its prey will dart and dodge to try to escape. The cheetah has to be able to make turns, too. It has claws that stick out to provide grip in high-speed turns. The cheetah's tail has a flat surface, like the rudder of a boat, and this helps it to balance its body as it runs. There is another problem, however, and that is stopping. When the cheetah tackles its prey, it is travelling at full speed. It has to be able to stop quickly, otherwise its prey will get up and escape. It stops by slamming down its two front legs, which act like brakes on a car. Pointed pads on the back of the front legs tear into the ground, bringing the cheetah to an almost immediate halt. Then, it grabs its prey before it can get away. Once the prey is caught, the cheetah bites the underside of the throat, suffocating the animal. The prey is dragged away to shelter and eaten.

▼ This group of young cheetahs is learning how to hunt.

Classification key

ORDER	Carnivora
FAMILY	Felidae
GENUS	*Acinomyx*
SPECIES	***Acinomyx jubatus***

◀ The cheetah uses its tail to balance while running.

Communicating

▲ The howl of the male howler monkey carries for more than half a kilometre. The howls help the different troops (groups of monkeys) to keep in contact with each other in the forest.

Mammals have well-developed senses of sight, hearing, touch, smell and taste, which they use to communicate with each other and to explore their surroundings.

Importance of colour

Primates are the only mammals that can see in full colour. Rainforests are dark places and animals that are brown or black cannot be seen easily, so some monkeys use colour to communicate. Colour helps the different **species** to identify one another. Mandrills have a bright-coloured face with red nose and blue cheeks, while the uakari has a bald, red head and face.

Sound and smell

Many mammals live in specific areas, called **territories**, which they defend against intruders. Sound can be important in telling would-be intruders that the territory has an owner, for example the roaring of lions and tigers. Some mammals mark the boundary of their territory with scent. These mammals have scent-producing **glands** around their face, feet or under the tail. Hyenas and lions use urine as a scent marker. They mark stones and trees along the edges of their territory, where the scent can be detected by others.

▼ A tiger sprays urine against a tree at nose height, so its scent is easily detected by other tigers.

Echolocation and sonar

Some mammals use sound to help them find their way around. Bats use a special system called echolocation. The bat produces a high-pitched sound in its larynx (voice box), which is emitted through the nose or mouth. These sounds bounce off objects in front of the bat. The returning echoes are picked up by the specialized ears of the bat. The echoes tell the bat about the position of objects, such as **prey**, in its path.

▼ Dolphins communicate with each other using chirping, whistling and squeaking sounds.

Amazing facts

- A dolphin can emit as many as 2000 clicks per second.
- Bush babies urinate on their hands and feet, so that when they climb around the forest they leave behind a trail of scent.
- White rhinos stamp in their dung to spread their own smell with each step.

Dolphins also use sound to help detect prey while swimming. This is a type of sonar, similar to that used by submarines. The dolphin produces a series of low- and high-pitched clicks. When any of these clicks hit an object the sound waves they produce bounce back to the dolphin. The high-pitched clicks provide information about objects that are close by, for example the size and type of a nearby fish. Low-pitched clicks travel further, and help a dolphin locate and identify objects that are further away.

Living together

Some **mammals** live alone, a few mammals live with a partner, but many live together in groups. These groups may stay together permanently or just for short periods of time. Some groups may be all males or all females while others include both sexes. Mammals that live on their own, such as the aardvark, usually only meet up with others to **mate**. Gibbons live in pairs and look after their young until they are old enough to survive on their own.

Living in groups

There are advantages for mammals that live in a group rather than on their own, especially for the smaller mammals. In a group it is more likely that **predators** will be spotted, so there is a greater chance of escape. Living in a group also makes it easier to protect a **territory** against intruders. Some mammals help each other to raise the young, so more will survive and grow to adulthood. For example, meerkats live in groups of up to 30. One or two meerkats climb up on to mounds or bushes to watch for predators, while the others feed. They gang up together to chase away some predators.

Amazing facts

- Prairie dogs live in huge, underground burrows called cities. One of the largest cities found was in Texas, USA. It covered 64,000 square kilometres (24,500 square miles) and was believed to be home to 400 million prairie dogs.

- In Australia, fruit bats known as flying foxes roost together in trees. Up to 1 million may live in a 'camp'.

▲ When a troop of monkeys rests during the day, the monkeys often spend time grooming each other.

A pride of lions

Lions live in a group called a pride, consisting of up to twelve related lionesses, their young and between one and six males. Each pride lives in a territory, which they defend against other prides. There are many advantages to living in a pride. Hunting is more successful when it involves teamwork. It is also easier for them to steal **prey** from other **carnivores** and they can protect their kills from hyenas, too.

▲ Lionesses and their cubs watch over the savannah.

Elephant herds

Female elephants live with their offspring in a group called a herd. The herd is led by the oldest female, known as the matriarch. When they reach adulthood, young females stay with the herd but the males leave and either live alone or travel with other young males. Elephants are long lived and the matriarch may lead her herd for many years. The herd benefits from her years of experience of knowing where to find food and water, and how to avoid danger.

▼ Like elephants, wildebeest live in herds. This herd of wildebeest is crossing a river in search of fresh grazing areas.

Mammalian orders

The class of **mammals** is divided up into smaller groups, called sub-classes. There are three sub-classes within the class mammalia: the **monotremes** (Prototheria), **marsupials** (Theria) and **placental** mammals (Eutheria). The monotremes and marsupials are the two **primitive** groups, comprising 297 **species** in total. By far the largest sub-class is the placental mammals, with approximately 4332 species. The sub-classes are further divided into groups called orders. There are 21 different mammalian orders. Scientists called biologists study the features of the different mammals and place those with similar features into the same order.

► Meerkats are **carnivores**. They live in burrows under the ground and emerge each morning to hunt for prey.

Amazing facts

- The smallest mammal is the Kitti's hog-nosed bat, *Craseonycteris thonglongyai*, from Thailand. It is only 2.9–3.3 centimetres long and weighs less than 2 grams, which makes it smaller than many insects and snails.

- The largest land animal is the bull African elephant. The largest specimen recorded stood around 3.96 metres at the shoulder and weighed over 12 tonnes.

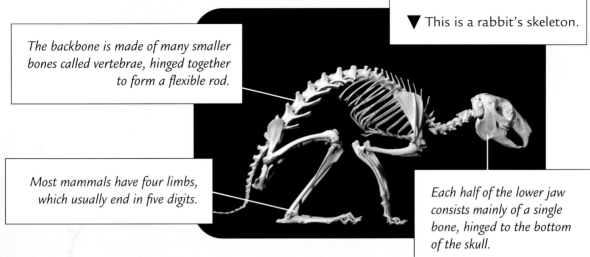

The backbone is made of many smaller bones called vertebrae, hinged together to form a flexible rod.

▼ This is a rabbit's skeleton.

Most mammals have four limbs, which usually end in five digits.

Each half of the lower jaw consists mainly of a single bone, hinged to the bottom of the skull.

Skeletal clues

In order to divide the placental mammals into different orders it is necessary to look at features such as their **skeleton**. **Primates** and insectivores have four limbs that end in five **digits** (fingers or toes). In some orders the limb has changed, or **evolved**, into a different shape. In the bat, the forelimb has four long fingers to support its wing. Whales and dolphins have short 'arms' and the digits form a flipper for swimming. They have lost their hind limbs. Some mammals have long legs that end in hooves. Hoofed mammals can be separated into two orders: those with an even number of toes such as deer (Artiodactyla), and those with an odd number such as zebras (Perissodactyla).

The skull

The skull of placental mammals is made up of about 34 bones, which are fused together. There are three parts: the cranium, which encloses the brain, the rostrum (snout and upper jaw) and the lower jaw. The lower jaw consists of just a single bone on either side, which hinges with the bottom of the cranium. A mammal's skull provides clues about its diet. Carnivores have forward-facing eye sockets, which enable them to judge distances and spot **prey**. They have sharp, pointed **canine** teeth, which are long and curved for stabbing. The skull of a **herbivore** has teeth that are **adapted** to tear up and chew plants, and large, sideways-facing eye sockets for a wide field of vision.

▼ Pangolins belong to the order Pholidota. They are covered in scales that give protection and camouflage.

Carnivores

▼ Large, sharp teeth allow these polar bears to make short work of their prey.

Carnivores are the hunters of the **mammal** world, **preying** on other animals. They vary in size, ranging from the large Kodiak bear (a type of brown bear) to the tiny weasel. Carnivores can be found in many different climates around the world. Polar bears and Arctic foxes are found in the Arctic, and there are carnivores in rainforests and deserts.

Teeth for stabbing

The teeth of the carnivores are **adapted** to their meat diet. Carnivores use their teeth to grip and kill their prey, and then to eat it. They have four long, curved **canine** teeth, two on the top jaw and two on the bottom jaw. These teeth are used to stab and hold on to prey. Towards the back of their mouth there are four large teeth known as the carnassials. These teeth are razor sharp, and they can slice through skin and muscle. Carnivores have powerful muscles to close their jaws. These muscles are essential as they help them to capture and tear up prey.

▼ African prairie dogs hunt in groups called packs. They hunt impala, antelopes, wildebeest and gazelles, usually picking out the youngest or weakest animals from a herd.

Catching prey

Carnivores find their prey using their well-developed senses of sight, hearing and smell. Many carnivores creep up on their prey and pounce when they are close. Some will chase their prey, for example the African wild dog or the cheetah (see pages 16–17). These carnivores have a flexible spine and long legs. Larger hunters, such as the lion and tiger, have powerful shoulders to pull down their prey, which is often much larger than themselves. Some kill their prey by biting through the neck or skull, while others suffocate their victims. Some carnivores, such as the wolf or the lion, hunt in groups to improve their chances of making a successful kill.

Amazing facts

- Unlike other carnivores, the giant panda feeds mainly on bamboo shoots and roots, as well as just a few insects.
- The sharp teeth and the strong jaw muscles of the spotted hyena enable it to crush bones, and to rip through tough skin and tendons, which other carnivores cannot eat.
- The Kodiak bear is the world's largest land carnivore, weighing nearly half a tonne. Despite its size it can charge at speeds of up to 50 kilometres (30 miles) per hour.

Classification key

SUB-CLASS	Eutheria
ORDER	**Carnivora**
FAMILIES	7 (Cat, dog, bear, racoon, weasel, civet and hyena)
SPECIES	249

▲ The stoat may be one of the smaller carnivores, but it can kill large prey such as rabbits.

The tiger

The tiger is the largest of all the cats. It is a powerful animal with a muscular body, a large head and long **canine** teeth for stabbing **prey**. Tigers are found across central Asia, including China, India, Malaysia and Indonesia.

▲ Tigers may be large but they are agile, too. They can jump and swim and have been known to climb trees.

Tiger basics

Tigers live alone in their own **territory**. The size of a tiger's territory depends on the type of habitat it lives in and the numbers of prey animals available. Tigers are superb hunters, preying on large **mammals** such as wild boar, deer and even elephants. They hunt at night when their prey animals are most active. The tiger creeps up on its prey either from the side or from behind. It gets as close as possible before pouncing. The tiger grabs the prey using its teeth and claws. The weight of the tiger's body brings its victim crashing to the ground. Then it quickly grips its prey by the neck, blocking its windpipe, which suffocates it. With smaller prey, the tiger bites through the neck instead.

Classification key

SUB-CLASS	Eutheria
ORDER	Carnivora
FAMILY	Felidae
GENUS	*Panthera*
SPECIES	***Panthera tigris***
SUB-SPECIES	5 (see fact box on page 27)

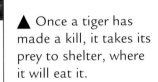

Female tigers give birth to up to three cubs. Tiger cubs are born blind and weigh only about 1 kilogram. They live on their mother's milk for six to eight weeks before they follow her on hunts and start to eat meat. They begin making their own kills when they are about eighteen months old. By the time they are two years old, the young tigers are ready to leave their mother.

▲ Once a tiger has made a kill, it takes its prey to shelter, where it will eat it.

Tigers under threat

Today, tigers are endangered mammals – there are barely 7000 tigers left in the wild. The number of tigers has fallen rapidly for various reasons. Their forest habitat has been cleared for farmland, timber and industry. Many tigers are killed because people are scared of them. Farmers shoot them to protect their livestock. One of the major threats comes from **poaching**. People kill tigers for their skin and bones, which can be used in traditional Chinese medicines.

▼ These tiger cubs will stay with their mother until they are two years old, when they will be powerful enough to hunt on their own.

Amazing facts – tiger sub-species

- Bengal – found in Indian forests and swamps, weighs up to 260 kilograms, up to 4700 left in the wild.
- Sumatran – the smallest tiger, found in forests of Sumatra, Indonesia, fewer than 500 in the wild.
- Indochinese – found in South-east Asia, up to 1500 left in the wild.
- Siberian – the biggest cat, weighing up to 350 kilograms, no more than 400 left in the wild and just under 500 in zoos.
- South China – the rarest tiger, weighing just 150 kilograms; there are fewer than 30 in the wild and 50 in zoos.

Primates

Primates are among the most familiar **mammals**, because they include humans, or *Homo sapiens*. Primates have much larger brains than other mammals in proportion to their body size and the largest brain is found in humans. The order is divided up into two sub-orders: the **primitive** prosimians and the more advanced anthropoids (monkeys and apes).

▲ Many primates live in South-east Asia, including apes such as orang-utans.

Grasping hands and feet

Most primates have fingers and toes that end in flat nails rather than claws. The apes have an 'opposable' big toe and thumb, which means that they can grasp objects. Sensitive pads on the underside of the fingers and toes help when gripping. Humans do not have the opposable big toe. Our thumbs are opposable, and can be rotated into a position opposite our fingers to give a powerful grip.

Classification key

SUB-CLASS	Eutheria
ORDER	**Primate**
FAMILIES	11
SPECIES	356

Amazing facts

- The smallest primate is the pygmy mouse lemur, which weighs around 30 grams.
- The largest is the gorilla, weighing up to 200 kilograms.
- In the forests of the Ivory Coast, west Africa, groups of chimpanzees work together to chase and kill monkeys for food.

Prosimians

The prosimians include lemurs, lorises and galagos. They are found mostly in forests. They are often nocturnal and have large, round eyes with good night vision. They have nails except for their second toe, which has a long claw, called a toilet claw. They have an unusual arrangement of teeth on the lower jaw, where four to six teeth are pressed together to form a dental 'comb', which is used for grooming, with the toilet claw.

▲ Lemurs, like all primates, have forward-facing eyes, which help them to judge distances as they travel from one place to another.

Monkeys and apes

Monkeys are forest dwellers, too. They move around the trees by running and leaping between branches. They have short, flat faces, a flexible spine and a flattened chest. They have legs that are longer than their arms and they walk on all fours, using their tail for balance. Some species have a **prehensile** tail, which acts like a fifth limb. The prehensile tail has muscles and can curl around branches, helping the monkey to move through the trees.

Apes include gibbons, orang-utans, chimpanzees, gorillas and humans. They have a shorter spine and broad hips that give a more upright posture. They have a broad chest and a shoulder joint that allows their arms to make a wide range of movements. Apes have flatter faces than monkeys and the lower jaw is quite prominent.

▼ The hands and feet of primates are described as dextrous, which means that they can be used to handle objects easily.

The gorilla

The gorilla is one of our closest relatives. It is the largest of the **primates**, reaching a height of just under 2 metres and weighing up to 200 kilograms. Gorillas walk on all fours, on the soles of their hind feet and on the knuckles of their hands.

There are two **species** of gorilla. The western gorilla is found in western and central Africa. About 100,000 still remain in tropical forests. The eastern gorilla is found in central and eastern Africa. There are three subspecies, the best known of which is the mountain gorilla. This gorilla has long shaggy fur, which keeps it warm high up in the mountains.

Classification key

SUB-CLASS	Eutheria
ORDER	Primate
FAMILY	Pongidae
GENUS	*Gorilla*
SPECIES	*Gorilla gorilla* (western gorilla) and *Gorilla beringei* (eastern gorilla)

Family groups

Gorillas live in family groups. A typical group of mountain gorillas is made up of one or two adult males aged twelve years or older (called silverbacks), several young males (called blackbacks), and a number of females, juveniles and infants. One of the oldest males is the dominant male and he leads the group in their search for food and protects them from dangers, such as other males. The dominant male will father most of the offspring in the group.

◀ When gorillas feel threatened, they make loud sounds, such as roars and screams. Facial expressions are also important in communication.

◀ An adult male gorilla is much larger than the females. He has a bony crest above his head and a band of silver-coloured fur across his back.

Gorilla females do not **mate** before they are about ten years old. They usually give birth to one baby, which they carry around for up to eight months. A female gorilla holds her newborn offspring close to her chest at first, but the infant soon learns how to hold on for itself. It rides on its mother's back until it is old enough to walk on its own. Female gorillas form a strong bond with their babies and stay with them for four years or more before giving birth again.

Gorilla food

Gorillas eat mostly leaves and stems rather than fruits. Sometimes they eat ants, as well as the occasional worm or grub. The mountain gorilla feeds almost entirely on giant celery, nettles and vines. It has to eat a lot of leaves each day because leaves are low in nutrients.

Amazing facts

- A fully-grown mountain gorilla eats 27 kilograms of vegetation a day.
- An older male is called a silverback because of the silver 'saddle' of hair on its back.
- The mountain gorilla is the most endangered species of gorilla, with barely 350 remaining in the mountains of Rwanda, Uganda and Zaire.

▼ This silverback male is leading a family group of other adults and youngsters.

Even-toed hoofed mammals

The most widespread of the large **herbivore mammals** belong to the order Artiodactyla. The word 'Artiodactyla' means 'even toes'. Artiodactyls usually have two large toes, forming a hoof on each leg, with two shorter toes on either side, which do not touch the ground. Sometimes these smaller toes are absent. The bones in the foot are long and the 'ankle' is located much higher up the leg, approximately where our knees are found. With fewer toes and longer legs, these mammals can run fast to escape **predators** such as lions and wolves. Although most artiodactyls are fast moving, hippos are slow and cumbersome.

▼ Reindeer have two large toes. Two shorter toes can be seen sticking out behind the hoof.

Feeding habits

Most artiodactyls are either **browsers** or **grazers**. Browsers feed on the leaves of trees and shrubs. A narrow muzzle and mobile lips allow them to pick off leaves. Grazers tend to feed on grasses. Pigs and peccaries root around in the ground using their long snouts and jaw muscles.

▼ Millions of artiodactyls are found on the savannah grasslands of southern Africa. Most live in groups or herds for safety.

▲ These two male springbok (small antelope) are fighting over females. They face each other head down, lock their antlers and push against each other.

Classification key

SUB-CLASS	Eutheria
ORDER	**Artiodactyla**
FAMILIES	10
SPECIES	220

Amazing facts

- The giraffe is the tallest animal, at 6 metres. It has an incredibly long neck, but like most other mammals it has only seven neck bones or vertebrae.
- The okapi has a long, black tongue that can curl around leaves and branches and pull them into its mouth.
- The musk ox is named after the strong smell given off by the male during the **mating** season. The males fight over the females by charging at each other with their heads down.

Most of these mammals are **ruminants** – animals that chew the cud. Ruminants have stomachs that consist of either three or four chambers. The food goes into the first chamber, called the rumen, which contains millions of bacteria that help to digest the food. Then the animal **regurgitates** the food back into its mouth to chew it again. This softens and breaks up the food so it is digested more easily. Pigs and peccaries are **omnivorous**. They have a mixed diet and they do not ruminate.

Horns and antlers

Many artiodactyls have horns or antlers. Horns are bony outgrowths of the skull, which are covered with either keratin or skin. Most male deer have antlers rather than horns. Antlers are made of dead bone and they drop off at the end of each year and grow back the following year.

Odd-toed hoofed mammals

Odd-toed hoofed **mammals** are very similar to artiodactyls, except that they have an odd number of toes. The order is called Perissodactyla, and it includes horses, zebras, rhinos and tapirs. Horses and zebras have a single large toe, while rhinos and tapirs have three toes.

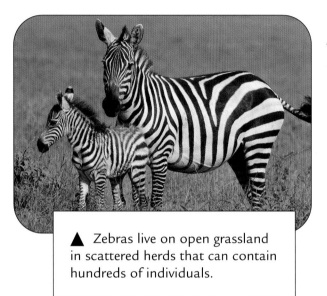

▲ Zebras live on open grassland in scattered herds that can contain hundreds of individuals.

Classification key

SUB-CLASS	Eutheria
ORDER	**Perissodactyla**
FAMILIES	3 (Equidae, Tapiridae, Rhinoceroridae)
SPECIES	78

Ancient horses

About 50 million years ago, a small **herbivore** with three toes walked on the North American grasslands. It was **preyed** upon by huge, wolf-like dogs and sabre-toothed cats, so it relied on speed to escape. This was the ancestor of the horse. Slowly, the middle toe evolved to become longer and wider, and formed a hoof while the other two toes became smaller. The legs got longer, too. Longer legs gave the horse a longer stride, so that it could run faster than its ancestors. In time, the animal took on the appearance of the modern horse. Donkeys and zebras then **evolved** from the horse.

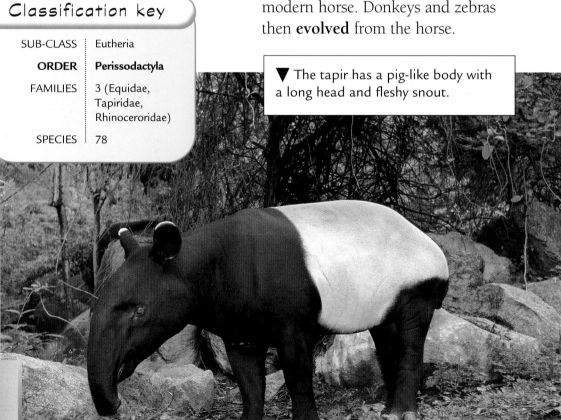

▼ The tapir has a pig-like body with a long head and fleshy snout.

Feeding

The perissodactyls are not **ruminants**, so most of the digestion of their food takes place in the hind gut. The hind gut is filled with millions of bacteria that help to digest plant food. The food does not stay in the stomach for very long, so perissodactyls can eat large quantities of food each day. They can also survive on poorer-quality grass than the artiodactyls.

Tapirs are forest dwellers, and they **browse** on leaves as well as a variety of fruits and nuts that they find on the forest floor. They have chisel-shaped incisors, which they use to snip off leaves, and ridged molars to grind them up.

The white and black rhinos look very similar, although their names suggest that they have different-coloured skin. The white rhino's name comes from the Afrikaans word *weit*, which means wide. This refers to its wide mouth for **grazing** on grass. Black rhinos have a pointed upper lip, which is ideal for browsing.

Amazing facts

- The zebra's stripes were once thought to be for camouflage but most biologists think that the stripes help zebras recognize, and stay close to, each other.
- One **extinct species** of rhinoceros, Indricotherium, was the largest land mammal that ever lived, standing approximately 5.4 metres tall at the shoulder and weighing around 30,000 kilograms – that is five times the weight of an elephant!
- Rhinos have the thickest skin of any land mammal. The skin on their backs and sides can be 2.5 centimetres thick.

▼ The white rhino has poor eyesight and relies on its sense of smell to find its way around.

Elephants, hyraxes, aardvarks and rabbits

There are a number of mammalian orders that contain just a few **species** and in one case, just a single species. Aardvarks, elephants and hyraxes are closely related to the even- and odd-toed **mammals** (see pages 32–35), while rabbits are related to rodents (see pages 38–39). All these mammals are **herbivores**.

Amazing facts

- An elephant's tusks grow throughout its life and can reach lengths of 3.5 metres.
- Despite their size, elephants can walk silently through the savannah and hardly leave any tracks.
- An elephant's skin is thick but very sensitive. It needs frequent baths and powdering with dust to keep it free from parasites and disease.

Classification key

SUB-CLASS	Eutheria
ORDER	**Proboscidea**
SPECIES	3

Elephants (Order Proboscidea)

There are three species of elephant, the African, African forest and Asian elephant. The African elephant is the largest living land animal, standing up to 4 metres high. Females normally weigh up to 3 tonnes and the males up to 6 tonnes. Elephants have large, flapping ears and a long trunk, which is an extension of the upper lip and nose. The elephant uses its trunk like an arm to feed, reaching up into trees to pull off leaves, and to throw water and dust over itself. Elephants have large, upper incisors called tusks. Their skin is thick, wrinkled and has very few hairs.

▼ Elephants use their trunks to drink and throw water over themselves.

Hyraxes (Order Hyracoidea)

Hyraxes are small mammals that are closely related to elephants. They are found in central and southern Africa and parts of the Middle East. The pads of their feet are sticky and this helps them to climb rocks and trees. The rock hyrax lives in rocky outcrops, while the tree hyrax is found among trees and shrubs. These mammals are survivors, able to feed on the toughest of plants, and can live on very little water.

Classification key

SUB-CLASS	Eutheria
ORDER	**Hyracoidea**
SPECIES	11

Aardvarks (Order Tubulidentata)

The aardvark is an African mammal with a long nose, large ears and a body like a pig. It has excellent senses of smell and hearing to find termites and ants, which it digs out with its long claws. It licks up the insects with its long, sticky tongue.

▼ The aardvark has long ears for hearing and a large snout for sniffing out its favourite food – ants.

Classification key

SUB-CLASS	Eutheria
ORDER	**Tubulidentata**
SPECIES	1

▼ The winter coat of the Arctic hare is white to blend in with the snow. Its long ears have black tips.

Rabbits, hares and pikas (Order Lagomorpha)

Rabbits, hares and pikas are found across the world. Like rodents, they have a pair of large incisors, but they have a second pair, too, just behind the upper incisors. These are called peg teeth. The lagomorphs are **grazing** mammals, spending much of the day feeding on a variety of plants. Rabbits and hares have long back legs that allow them to run fast. Hares can reach speeds of up to 56 kilometres (35 miles) per hour.

Classification key

SUB-CLASS	Eutheria
ORDER	**Lagomorpha**
SPECIES	58

Rodents

Rodents are small **mammals**, often with long tails, clawed feet and chisel-like teeth for gnawing. Rodents are among the most widespread orders of mammals and they are found all over the world, with the exception of Antarctica. Many have moved into our towns and cities, where they feed on food waste and live in our buildings and sewers.

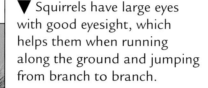

▼ Squirrels have large eyes with good eyesight, which helps them when running along the ground and jumping from branch to branch.

Chisel teeth

Rodents have a pair of razor-sharp incisors that in many species can even gnaw through wood. They do not have any **canine** teeth but they have premolars and molars to grind their food. Gnawing through tough plant material blunts their teeth, so their incisors are self-sharpening. Their incisors are arranged so that the top and bottom incisors grind against each other, sharpening the tooth into a cutting edge. Their incisors and cheek teeth continue to grow from the bottom throughout their life. This is essential to replace the tooth, which is worn away at the top.

Classification key

SUB-CLASS	Eutheria
ORDER	**Rodentia**
SUB-ORDERS	3 (Sciuromorpha, squirrel-like; Myomorpha, mouse-like; and Caviomorpha, cavy-like)
FAMILIES	30
SPECIES	1702

Amazing facts

- Not all rodents are small: the capybara from South America weighs up to 66 kilograms.
- Beavers are extreme gnawers, chiselling their way through whole tree trunks to build dams to flood valleys. Then they build a lodge with an underground opening.
- Rats are responsible for the spread of disease. Between 1347 and 1350, one in every three people in Europe died from the Black Death, or bubonic plague. It was spread by rats carrying fleas infected by the disease.

Fast breeders

Rodents breed fast and can give birth to several large litters each year, so their numbers increase rapidly. Around the world, huge numbers of rats and mice destroy crops, invade grain stores and carry disease.

▲ A female rat can **mate** when she is just two months old and can give birth to up to eleven young.

Squirrels, mice and cavies

Almost 40 per cent of all mammals are rodents. This large order is split into three sub-orders, the squirrel-like, mouse-like and cavy-like rodents. This is based on the arrangement of the jaw muscles, which means that each group has a slightly different type of bite. Squirrel-like rodents tend to have long, slim bodies and hairy tails, which they use for balance. This group includes beavers, marmots and prairie dogs. Mouse-like rodents are generally small with a pointed face and long whiskers, such as hamsters, rats, voles and lemmings. Cavy-like rodents are generally larger than the other rodents, with large heads and sturdy bodies. These rodents include guinea pigs, porcupines, capybaras and chinchillas.

▼ The porcupine has long spines along its back. When attacked, it raises its spines and charges backwards at any **predator**.

Insect eaters

▲ The desman has a snout that is elongated into a kind of snorkel so that it can breathe while under water.

The insect eaters belong to the order Insectivora. They are small, nocturnal **mammals** with well-developed senses to find their **prey**. Although they are called insectivores, or insect eaters, they eat other small **invertebrates** such as worms and slugs. Most insectivores live on land but some have **adapted** to living near water, for example the web-footed tenrec.

Long snouts

Insectivores tend to have a small face with beady eyes. Their most noticeable feature is a long, slim snout, which they use to find prey. The weird-looking solenodon has a particularly long snout, which is very flexible and can be pushed into cracks to find prey. Insectivores have small but sharp teeth, and each foot has five clawed toes. Most insectivores live alone and they are found all over the world except for Australia and New Zealand.

Some insectivores have unusual features. The hedgehog and tenrec have spines for protection. The mole has extra-large front paws for digging, while the solenodon and some shrews produce a poisonous **saliva**.

▼ The European mole spends its life underground. It digs a network of tunnels using its spade-like front feet, only occasionally popping up to the surface.

40

Classification key

SUB-CLASS	Eutheria
ORDER	**Insectivora**
FAMILIES	6
SPECIES	365

Amazing facts

- The Etruscan, or pygmy white-toothed shrew is the world's smallest land mammal: even when fully grown it can sit in a teaspoon.

- The star-nosed mole of North America is a strange-looking insectivore. It has a pink fleshy star attached to the tip of its nose, which can find and identify up to five different invertebrates in less than one second.

- Young shrews are led around by their mother in a long chain, each holding on to the shrew in front. This is called a caravan.

▲ Although they are small, shrews can be quite aggressive and tackle large prey such as earthworms.

Tiny shrews

There are 300 different species of shrew and most are smaller than a mouse. One of their big problems is that they lose heat very quickly, so they have to eat constantly in order to stay warm. Some eat as much as three times their own body weight in food each day! Many shrews live among fallen leaves on the ground, where it is quite dark, and they rely on their sense of touch and smell to find food. Shrews also use sound to find their way around, making high-pitched squeaks, which we cannot hear, and listening to the echoes that bounce off objects.

Cetaceans

Cetaceans include whales and dolphins. They are **mammals** that have **adapted** to live an aquatic lifestyle, even giving birth in water.

Streamlined shape

Cetaceans have torpedo-shaped bodies that are wide in front and gradually become narrower towards the tail. Unlike other mammals, cetaceans have no hair, so the surface of their skin is very smooth. Their front 'limbs' are flippers and they have no hind limbs. Their tails have a unique shape with two horizontal extensions, called flukes. The flukes force the animal through the water and provide tremendous swimming power.

▲ When a whale breathes out, a column of warm air and water is forced out of the blow-hole on the top of its head. This adult bule whale and its calf are shown from above.

Amazing facts

- The blue whale is the largest animal. It is 24–27 metres long and weighs a massive 130–150 tonnes – equivalent to 33 of the largest elephants.
- In 1930–31 in the Southern Ocean more than 31,000 blue whales were hunted by European whalers. Today the population is just 6000.
- The sperm whale can dive to depths of 1000 metres and can stay under water for as long as 90 minutes.

Breathing air

Fish breathe under water using gills, but cetaceans have lungs and they have to swim to the surface of the water to breathe air. However, they can stay underwater for 20 or 30 minutes, sometimes longer. They make each lungful of air last much longer by slowing down the rate at which their heart beats. At great depths their lungs can be completely squashed to absorb the last bit of available oxygen.

Classification key

SUB-CLASS	Eutheria
ORDER	**Cetacea**
SUB-ORDERS	2 (Mysticeti, or baleen whales, and Odontoceti, or toothed whales)
FAMILIES	9
SPECIES	76

Baleen and toothed whales

The cetaceans are divided into two sub-orders, baleen whales (Mysticeti) and toothed whales (Odontoceti). Baleen whales are the giant whales such as humpback, blue and grey whales. They are filter feeders and their name comes from the huge baleen plates in their mouths that filter out food from the water. They swallow a large mouthful of water, which is forced through the baleen plates, trapping food such as plankton, krill and even fish. The toothed whales include dolphins, porpoises, killer whales, white whales, sperm whales and beaked whales. As their name suggests, they all have teeth. They each have a fluid-filled swelling on the forehead called a melon, with a beak in front of it. The toothed whales are hunters, feeding mostly on fish and squid. The killer whale, or orca, even hunts other whales.

► The killer whale, or orca, has a powerful tail to propel it at speed through the water. Its tall dorsal fin, seen sticking out of the water, provides balance.

▲ Dolphins leap out of water when they are being playful, but they also do this to attract other dolphins when they have found a shoal of fish to eat.

The humpback whale

The humpback whale is a baleen whale. It grows to 16 metres long and weighs up to 65 tonnes. Humpback whales feed on krill (small, shrimp-like crustaceans) and small fish. They do not have any teeth. Instead they have up to 400 fringed baleen plates, which hang from the upper jaw. During feeding, the pleated grooves in the throat expand so the whale can swallow a huge mouthful of water and food. When the mouth closes, water is forced out through the plates. The food trapped inside is then swallowed.

A humpback's year

Humpback whales spend the months of June to October feeding in cold waters, such as the Arctic and Southern Oceans, where food is plentiful. Then the whales **migrate** to warmer waters in November, where they stay until February. Here they give birth to their calves. They return to cold waters with their calves between March and June. The calves are fed on milk that is rich in fat until they are one year old. This helps the calf to build up a thick layer of **blubber**, which will enable the calf to survive in cold water.

▲ These whales are feeding. They scoop large mouthfuls of food and water, and filter it through their baleen plates (the pink area of the photo).

The song of the humpback

Male humpbacks are famous for the sounds they make, or their songs. Each song is made up of different sounds such as yups, snores, groans, ees, oohs and chirps. The song can last up to 35 minutes and forms part of a song session that may go on all day and night. Each individual's song changes over time as new bits are added or removed. No one is sure of the significance of the song. It could be to attract females or to communicate with other whales.

◀ A female whale gives birth to a single calf every two to three years.

Whaling

Humpback whales are slow swimmers and their migration routes take them close to shore. Historically, this made the humpbacks easy to hunt. Between 1905 and 1965, about 28,000 humpback whales were killed. In 1966 the whales came under the protection of The International Whaling Commission (IWC). Today, there are about 20,000 humpbacks – one-fifth of the population in 1905.

Amazing facts

- The migration of the humpback is one of the longest known in the animal kingdom. The whales of the Northern Pacific swim from south-eastern Alaska to Hawaii and back each year, a distance of 9400 kilometres (5800 miles).

- A humpback whale calf is between 3 and 4.5 metres long at birth and weighs about 900 kilograms.

- Each whale eats up to 1350 kilograms of food a day.

◀ Humpback whales can throw themselves out of the water completely (breaching) and swim on their backs with their flippers in the air.

Classification key

SUB-CLASS	Eutheria
ORDER	Cetacea
SUB-ORDERS	Mysticeti
FAMILY	Balaenidae
GENUS	*Megaptera*
SPECIES	***Megaptera novaeangliae***

45

Seals, sea lions and sea cows

Whales and dolphins are not the only marine **mammals**. There are two other orders of marine mammals – Pinnipedia (seals and sea lions) and Sirenia (sea cows).

Seals and sea lions (Order Pinnipedia)

The pinnipeds include seals, sea lions and walruses. Their name comes from two Latin words, which mean 'wing-footed' mammals. The pinnipeds have **adapted** to a life in water. They have a **streamlined** body with powerful flippers and they can stay under water for up to 60 minutes. However, they return to land to give birth to their young. Seals and sea lions are covered in hair, but the walrus is hairless. Pinnipeds are meat eaters, and for this reason many biologists think that they should be classified with the **carnivores**.

The pinnipeds are divided into three families, the true seals, the eared seals and the walruses. True seals have no external ear flaps and have sleek fur. Their back flippers point backwards. They are particularly clumsy on land as they cannot raise their body up on to their front flippers. The eared seals include sea lions and fur seals. They have small external ears. They are far more agile on land since their front flippers can lift the upper body clear of the ground. The back flippers can be twisted so they lie under the body and can be used to push the animal forwards. The most **characteristic** feature of the walrus is its long pair of white tusks. Walruses have stout bodies with a thick layer of **blubber**, which helps them to survive in the cold waters of the Arctic, where they live.

▲ This Galapagos sea lion is chasing a puffer fish. Sea lions and fur seals have an external ear.

Classification key

SUB-CLASS	Eutheria
ORDER	**Pinnipedia**
SPECIES	33
ORDER	**Sirenia**
SPECIES	4

▲ True seals, such as this northern elephant seal, do not have any external ears. While clumsy on land, they are very graceful in the water.

Amazing facts

- When the walrus gets too hot, the blood vessels in the skin enlarge, giving the animal a brick-red appearance.
- The largest pinniped is the southern elephant seal. The bull seals can weigh as much as 3500 kilograms.

Dugongs and manatees (Order Sirenia)

Dugongs and manatees are large mammals that resemble seals. They are often referred to as 'sea cows'. These aquatic mammals live in warm, shallow waters, coming up to the surface to breathe every 20 minutes or so. They have fat and hairless bodies, between 2.5 and 4 metres long. Their front limbs are like paddles but they have no hind limbs. Spade-like tails push them through the water. Manatees are found in the swamps of the Amazon, Florida and the Caribbean. The dugong is found in the South-west Pacific and Indian Oceans. They feed mainly on plants.

▲ Manatees (or sea cows) live in shallow water and swim slowly along the bottom in search of food.

The minor orders

The orders of **mammals** covered on this page are less well known than the others and they contain some very strange-looking mammals.

Flying lemurs (Order Dermoptera)

Flying lemurs are mammals that look a bit like bats. They have skin that stretches out between neck, fingers and toes, enabling them to glide from tree to tree. They cannot fly, only glide and they are not lemurs. They are found in the forests of South-east Asia.

Classification key	
SUB-CLASS	Eutheria
ORDER	**Dermoptera**
SPECIES	2

Elephant shrews (Order Macroscelidea)

Elephant shrews get their name from their long, pointed snouts. They have a pair of long, powerful back legs for running. They are found in east Africa on grassland, in forest and even among rocky outcrops.

Classification key	
SUB-CLASS	Eutheria
ORDER	**Macroscelidea**
SPECIES	15

Tree shrews (Order Scandentia)

These are small, squirrel-like mammals that live on the ground, not in trees. They have thick, bushy tails and feet with sharp claws. They have no whiskers and rely on their senses of hearing, smell and sight to find **prey** in the rainforests of South-east Asia.

Classification key	
SUB-CLASS	Eutheria
ORDER	**Scandentia**
SPECIES	18

◀ Tree shrews have a pointed snout and large eyes.

Classification key

SUB-CLASS	Eutheria
ORDER	**Xenarthra**
SPECIES	29

▲ The thick coat of the sloth is home to many animals including mites and insects.

▲ The giant anteater has a small face with a long snout and long, powerful claws for ripping open termite mounds.

Classification key

SUB-CLASS	Eutheria
ORDER	**Pholidota**
SPECIES	7

Classification key

SUB-CLASS	Eutheria
ORDER	**Chiroptera**
SPECIES	951

Anteaters, sloths and armadillos (Order Xenarthra)

These mammals are grouped together because they have unusual joints in their backbones, a relatively small brain and few, if any, teeth. Armadillos and anteaters are insectivores, feeding on ants and termites. Anteaters have a long, tubular nose and long claws. Their bodies are covered in thick hair. The armadillo has an armour-like covering of hardened skin. Sloths are **herbivores** and eat leaves and fruits. The sloth spends its life in the trees and uses its long, curved claws to hang from branches. Sloths move very, very slowly.

Pangolins (Order Pholidota)

The pangolin has an armour-like body covering like the armadillo, but it is made of horny scales rather than skin. Pangolins have no teeth, and a long, sticky tongue that is ideal for licking up ants and termites. They roll up into a ball when threatened.

Bats (Order Chiroptera)

Bats are the only mammals to have true flapping wings and the ability to fly rather than glide. The wings extend from the legs and side of the body to the arms, held out by four slender fingers. The knee and foot bend in the opposite direction from other mammals. There are two types of bat, the small insect eaters (see photograph, page 14) and the larger fruit bats.

Marsupials

Marsupials are **mammals** that raise their young inside a pouch. They include kangaroos, koalas, wallabies and opossums. There are just under 300 different **species** and most of them are found in Australia and South America.

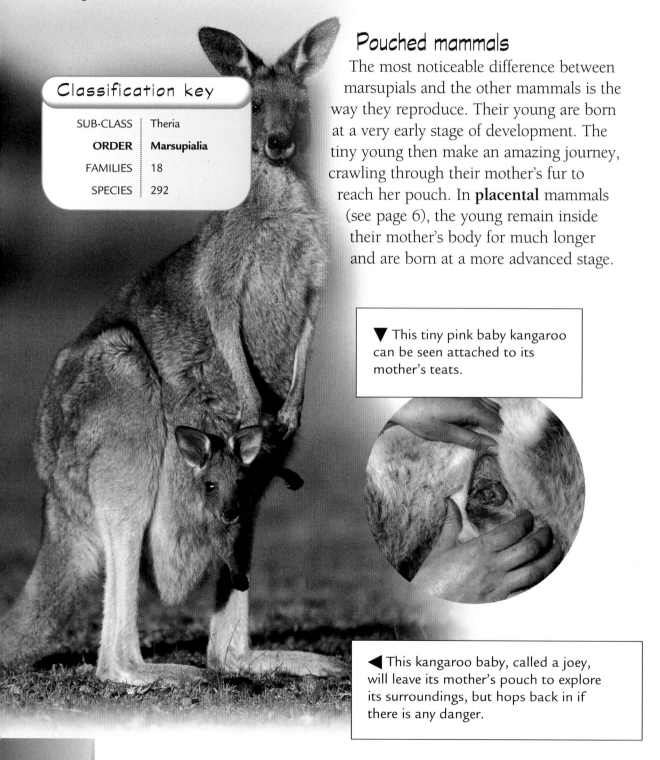

Classification key

SUB-CLASS	Theria
ORDER	**Marsupialia**
FAMILIES	18
SPECIES	292

Pouched mammals

The most noticeable difference between marsupials and the other mammals is the way they reproduce. Their young are born at a very early stage of development. The tiny young then make an amazing journey, crawling through their mother's fur to reach her pouch. In **placental** mammals (see page 6), the young remain inside their mother's body for much longer and are born at a more advanced stage.

▼ This tiny pink baby kangaroo can be seen attached to its mother's teats.

◄ This kangaroo baby, called a joey, will leave its mother's pouch to explore its surroundings, but hops back in if there is any danger.

▲ The koala is a specialized climber with short, muscular legs and feet that can grip tree trunks. It feeds almost entirely on the leaves of gum trees.

Most marsupials have a pouch. This is a fold of skin on the front of the female's **abdomen**. In koalas the pouch is a simple fold, while kangaroos and wallabies have a deep, pocket-like pouch. The teats are found inside the pouch, so the young animal does not have to leave the safety of the pouch to feed. As soon as it reaches the pouch, it sucks a teat, and stays attached for a couple of months until it is able to open its mouth and let go. At this point it may leave the pouch, but it continues to suckle milk for several months. A young red kangaroo spends seven months in its mother's pouch. It is fully independent of its mother by the time it is one year old.

Millions of years ago, Australia became cut off from the rest of the world. Placental mammals could not reach Australia, so marsupials remained the dominant mammals there. Marsupials are very varied and they are found in a wide range of habitats. There are marsupial examples of **herbivores**, **omnivores** and **carnivores**. There is a marsupial mole, a nectar-feeding honey possum and the wombat, which is the size of a European badger. There was even a marsupial wolf called the thylacine, but it is now **extinct**.

Amazing facts

- About 50,000 years ago there were giant kangaroos that stood 3 metres high and **browsed** on trees.
- The saying 'playing possum' comes from the habit of the Virginia possum, which is found in North America. When in danger it collapses and lies motionless on the ground for several hours, pretending to be dead, before jumping up and running away!

Monotremes

Of all of the **mammals** alive today, the most **primitive** are the **monotremes** – the egg-laying mammals. There are five **species** of monotremes and they are found only in Australia and New Guinea.

Egg laying is not the only unusual feature of this order. The monotremes do not have teeth – instead, they have a mouth like a beak. They grind their food between plates or spines in the mouth. Female monotremes feed their young milk, just like all the other mammals, but they do not have teats. The milk oozes from **glands** under a patch of fur on the chest.

▲ The short-beaked echidna has a curved snout and long spines. It uses its sense of smell to find ants and termites.

Echidnas

The echidna looks like a fat hedgehog with a small, hairy face, beady eyes and a long, pointed nose. It has curved claws to rip open the nests of termites and ants. Its body temperature is just 32° Celsius – that is 5° below that of humans. Echidnas can only just manage to generate enough body heat to stay alive.

▼ The long-beaked echidna is covered with fur and short spines. It has short legs and powerful claws.

The echidna has a strange courtship ritual. The female produces a strong smell that attracts males. Several males follow the female around for up to four weeks. They dig a trench in the ground and then they start fighting. They headbutt each other until one male remains in the trench. This is the male that **mates** with the female! Four weeks later, the female lays a small, leathery egg, the size of a grape. The egg sticks to a patch of hair in a simple pouch on her front and it stays there for ten days until the baby hatches.

The platypus

The platypus looks like a cross between a bird and a mammal, with its furry body, duck-like beak and webbed feet. The thick covering of fur keeps it warm in water. It shuts its eyes while underwater and uses its beak to find shrimps and molluscs on the riverbed. It stores the food in a cheek pouch before returning to its burrow to eat. A female platypus does not have a pouch. She lays two eggs and then wraps herself around the eggs to keep them warm. About eleven days later they hatch.

Amazing platypus facts

- A platypus can collect half its body weight in food in a single night.
- Male platypuses have spurs on their back legs that release a poison.

▼ The platypus has a slim body that ends in a flat, fur-covered tail. The webbed feet act as paddles.

Conservation

Mammals around the world are under threat. Well-known mammals such as the tiger and gorilla may become **extinct** in the wild in the next ten years. **Primates** are under the greatest threat, with more than 40 **species** in danger of extinction.

The main threat comes from the clearance of forests and other habitats by humans. Tropical rainforests are home to a huge range of plants and animals, but this habitat is disappearing at an ever-increasing rate. The trees are felled for timber or fuel wood, or to make way for new farmland, roads or industry. When the trees go the animals lose their homes. Most primates live in tropical forests so it is not surprising that the destruction of the rainforests is putting them at risk.

Amazing facts

- Since people started keeping records, 86 species and 24 subspecies of mammals have already become extinct.
- The International Union for the Conservation of Nature and Natural Resources (IUCN) publishes a 'red list' of species under threat. More than 25 per cent of all living mammals are on this list.

▼ The snow leopard has pale grey and white fur, which was highly prized by the fur trade. Today only a few hundred survive in the mountains of central Asia.

Hunting and whaling

Hunting is also a major threat. For many years big cats, such as tigers and leopards, were hunted for their fur, elephants were killed for their ivory, and rhinos were killed for their horns. Today, tigers are hunted for their bones, which are considered (wrongly) to have medicinal value. In central Africa, primates such as chimpanzees, bonobos and gorillas are hunted for meat. This is known as 'bush meat'. These primates often carry diseases, which humans can catch if they eat the meat.

Marine mammals have fared no better. Whales have been hunted close to extinction. Commercial whaling was finally banned in 1986 and their numbers have started to increase again. Now, however, whales and dolphins are under threat from overfishing. These mammals rely mostly on fish and krill for food, but as people overfish the oceans, there is less food for other animals.

▲ Among the souvenirs on sale in this east African shop is a leopard skin.

▲ Sperm whales were once hunted for their oil. When the whale is hauled out of the water it is stripped of its skin and **blubber**.

Marsupial decline

Some mammals are under threat because their habitat has been invaded by other mammals. The **marsupials** in Australia survived for millions of years without competition from other types of mammals. When Europeans arrived in Australia more than 200 years ago, they brought with them mice, rats, cats and dogs. These mammals spread across Australia and competed with the marsupials for food and space. Many marsupials could not survive and died out. Now there are overwhelming numbers of rabbits and mice in some parts of Australia, and they have to be controlled.

Protecting mammals

Many **mammals** are in danger of **extinction**, so it is vitally important that they are protected. Around the world, conservation organizations and national governments are working hard to find ways of ensuring their survival.

Amazing facts

- There were just 200 golden lion tamarins in the rainforests of Brazil during the 1970s. Conservation of its forests has lead to its recovery and in 2001 the population reached 1000.

- The Californian grey whale was hunted almost to extinction. Once whaling was banned the species recovered and now there are more than 17,000 individuals.

- The Antarctic fur seal was hunted for its fur during the 19th century and only a handful survived. It was given protection and now there are more than 1.5 million living on islands around the Antarctic.

▼ Millions of bison, or buffalo, once roamed the North American plains, but they were hunted almost to extinction. Yellowstone National Park, USA, is one of the few places where wild herds still survive.

Protecting habitats

It is impossible to protect an individual **species** without protecting its habitat. Animals and plants are dependent on each other so they all have to be protected. For example, the giant panda depends on the forests where the bamboo plants grow. Without the forests the pandas will not survive. One of the most important habitats to conserve is the tropical rainforest. Some countries have established huge national parks to protect what remains of their forests. The golden lion tamarin needs a rainforest habitat. Although this monkey **breeds** well in zoos it can only be reintroduced to the wild if its habitat still remains.

Breeding in zoos

Sometimes the only way to save a species from extinction is to keep breeding groups of animals in zoos and wildlife parks. Przewalski's horse survives only in captivity. If this horse had not been kept in zoos it would have become extinct. Père David's deer was saved by captive breeding in deer parks in the UK. It has now been reintroduced to its natural habitat in China.

▲ Giant pandas feed almost entirely on bamboo shoots. The forests in which the bamboo grows are declining and this is threatening the remaining pandas.

Wildlife tourism

Tourism can benefit wildlife. Many people enjoy watching wildlife and they will pay to go on holidays where they can see wildlife. Local communities around the world are realising that it is important to protect animals and their habitats. The tourists bring new jobs and money into an area. This money can be used to build schools and hospitals. However, the tourism has to be sustainable. This means the number of tourists has to be controlled. Too many tourists can lead to destruction of habitats. If the animals disappear, the tourists will stop visiting.

▶ Tourism can help conservation. Without the large mammals, few people would visit parts of Africa. Money from tourism can also help the local people.

Classification

Scientists have found and classified about 2 million different types of animal. With so many **species** it is important that they are classified into groups so that they can be described more accurately. The groups show how living **organisms** are related by **evolution** and where they belong in the natural world. A scientist identifies an animal by looking at its features, for example, by counting the number of legs or what teeth it has. Animals that share the same **characteristics** belong to the same species. Species with similar characteristics are placed in the same genus. The genera are grouped together in families, families are grouped into orders and orders are grouped into classes. Classes are grouped together in phyla (singular phylum) and finally, phyla are grouped into kingdoms. Kingdoms are the largest groups. There are five kingdoms: monerans (bacteria), protists (single-celled organisms), fungi, plants and animals.

Naming an animal

Each species has a unique Latin name consisting of two words. The first word is the name of the genus to which the organism belongs and the second is the name of its species. For example the Latin name of the lion is *Panthera leo* and that of the tiger is *Panthera tigris*. This tells us that these animals are grouped in the same genus but are different species. Many animals are given common names, but this may vary in different parts of the world. For example, *Alces alces* is called the moose in North America and the elk in Europe.

▼ The Bengal tiger is a sub-species of the tiger.

Sometimes there are very small differences between individuals that belong to the same species. So there is an extra division called a sub-species. To show that an animal belongs to a sub-species, another name is added to the end of the Latin name, for example the tiger has five sub-species, one of which is the Bengal tiger, *Panthera tigris tigris*.

This table shows how a blue whale is classified.

Classification	Example: blue whale	Features
Kingdom	Animalia	Whales belong to the kingdom Animalia because whales have many cells, need to eat food, and are formed from a **fertilized** egg.
Phylum	Chordata	An animal from the phylum Chordata has a strengthening rod called a notocord running down its back.
Sub-phylum	Vertebrata	Animals that have a backbone, a series of small bones running down the back, enclosing the spinal cord. The backbone replaces the notocord.
Class	Mammalia	Mammals provide milk for their young. They are **endothermic** and usually have a covering of hair.
Sub-class	Eutheria (live young)	The whale gives birth to live young. Whales are **placental** mammals.
Order	Cetacea	Cetaceans are mammals that live completely in water.
Sub-order	Mysticeti	Whales of the sub-order Mysticeti have baleen plates rather than teeth.
Family	Balaenidae	Members of the family Balaenidae have grooves around their throat that allow them to hold lots of water.
Genus	*Balaenoptera*	A genus is a group of species that are more closely related to one another than any group in the family. The blue whale's genus is *Balaenoptera*.
Species	*musculus*	A species is a grouping of individuals that **interbreed** successfully. The blue whale species name is *musculus*.

Mammal evolution

The origins of **mammals** date back millions of years. One group of reptiles known as synapsids lived 300 million years ago. These reptiles gave rise to mammal-like reptiles called therapsids. Scientists believe that mammals **evolved** from this group of reptiles.

▼ The ancestors of elephants like this one, first appeared about 60 million years ago.

About 200 million years ago, the first mammals appeared. They were shrew-like in appearance and just a few centimetres long. At this time the world was dominated by the giant dinosaurs. The small mammals scuttled around, almost unseen, in the undergrowth of forests. These early mammals had one important advantage over the dinosaurs – they could keep their bodies warm through the night. This meant that they could hunt while the dinosaurs and other reptiles were inactive. However, it was not until 65 million years ago that mammals started to become widespread. A huge meteorite is believed to have crashed into the Earth, changing the global climate. The dinosaurs died out and mammals became the dominant land **vertebrates**.

During the age of the dinosaurs, many different groups of mammals evolved. However, large numbers of mammals became **extinct** at the end of the last Ice Age. This was a time of major climate change and mammals such as the giant mammoths and sabre-toothed tigers disappeared. Today, just three groups remain, the **monotremes**, **marsupials** and the **placental** mammals. The diagram on page 61 shows when the different groups of mammals evolved.

◄ These chacma baboons are placental mammals.

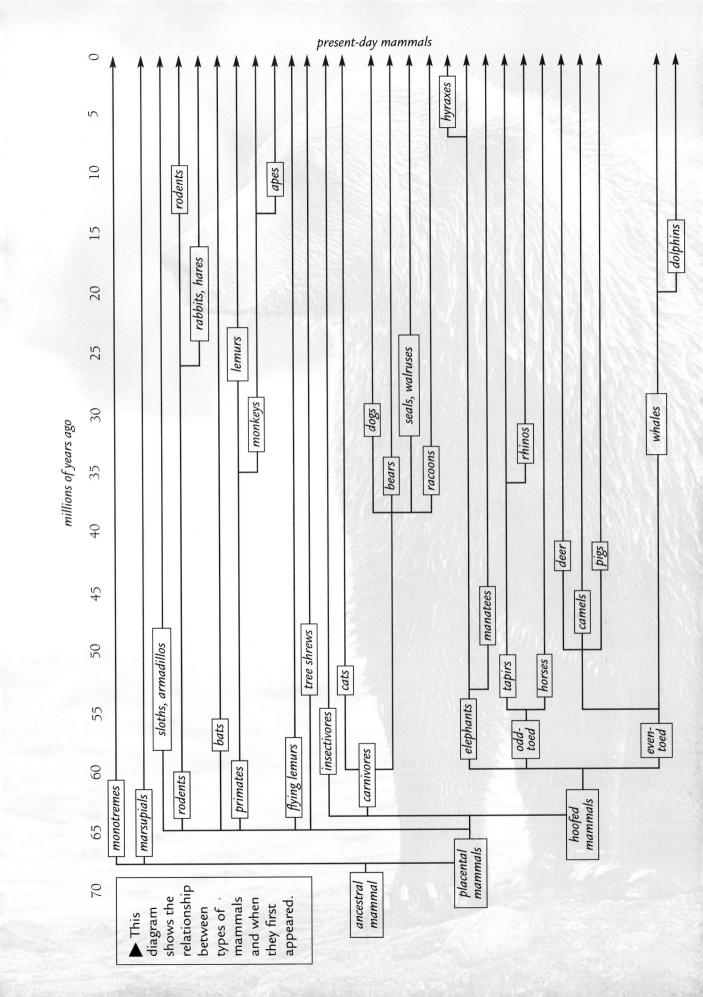

present-day mammals

millions of years ago

▲ This diagram shows the relationship between types of mammals and when they first appeared.

monotremes

marsupials

sloths, armadillos

rodents

rodents

bats

primates

lemurs

monkeys

apes

rabbits, hares

flying lemurs

tree shrews

insectivores

cats

carnivores

dogs

bears

seals, walruses

racoons

ancestral mammal

placental mammals

elephants

manatees

hoofed mammals

odd-toed

tapirs

rhinos

horses

even-toed

camels

deer

pigs

whales

dolphins

hyraxes

Glossary

abdomen lower part of a mammal's body that contains the gut, liver and kidneys

adapt change in order to cope with the environment

blubber thick layer of fat under the skin that helps mammals keep warm, found in marine mammals and polar bears

browser mammal that eats leaves from trees or bushes

canine tooth found at the front of the mouth; it is long and pointed in carnivores

carnivore mammal that hunts other mammals, for example cats and dogs

characteristic feature or quality of an animal, for example having hair or having wings

digit another name for a finger or toe

endothermy having a body temperature that is kept constant regardless of the temperature of the surroundings, also known as warm-blooded

evaporation change in state from liquid to gas, for example when water changes from a liquid to a vapour

evolution process of change in living organisms so they can adapt to their environment

evolve change very slowly over a long period of time

extinct no longer in existence

fertilize cause a female to produce young (an egg or live young) through the introduction of male reproductive material

gestation period time it takes from fertilization to birth of a young animal

gland organ that releases a substance such as saliva or sweat

graze to feed mainly on grass

herbivore mammal that eats plants

hibernation deep winter sleep

insulate keep warm

interbreed mate with another animal of the same species

invertebrate animal without a backbone

larva active, immature form of some animals before developing into adult form

mammal class of vertebrates that feed their young milk, are usually covered in hair and have a constant body temperature

mammary gland special gland on a female mammal that produces milk

manipulate handle or use an object in a skilful manner

marsupial pouched mammal. Marsupial babies are born at a very young stage and stay in their mother's pouch until they can move around on their own.

mate ability of male to fertilize the eggs of a female of the same species

membrane thin, flexible sheet

migrate regular journey made by an animal, often linked to the changes of the seasons

modified adapted or altered

monotreme egg-laying mammal

omnivore mammal that eats a mixed diet of plants and meat

organism any living thing

placenta area within the uterus through which food and oxygen pass from the mother's blood into the blood of the unborn baby

placental having the ability to nurture unborn young through the means of a placenta

poaching hunting animals for their horn, skin or meat

pouch fold of skin covering teats, found on the front of the abdomen of a female marsupial

predator animal that hunts other animals

prehensile part of the body that can wrap around objects to grip them, for example the tail of some monkeys and the trunk of an elephant

prey animal that is killed and eaten by other animals

primate mammal that belongs to the order primate, including lemurs, monkeys, apes and humans

primitive at an early stage of evolution or development. Monotremes are considered to be primitive mammals because they lay eggs.

regurgitate to bring the contents of the stomach back into the mouth in order to chew the food for a second time

ruminant hoofed mammal that has a three- or four-chambered stomach that contains bacteria that help to digest grass

saliva fluid produced in the mouth to help chew and digest food

skeleton bony framework of an animal

species group of individuals that share many characteristics and which can interbreed to produce offspring

streamlined slim shape that enables an animal or an object to move through water as easily as possible

territory range or area claimed by an animal or group of animals

uterus organ within a female mammal where an embryo, or immature young, develops before birth

vertebrate animal that has a backbone

Further information

BOOKS TO READ

Attenborough, David: *Life of Mammals* (BBC Books, 2002)

Burton, John: *Field Guide to the Mammals of Britain and Europe* (Kingfisher, 2002)

Macdonald, David (ed.): *The New Encyclopedia of Mammals* (Oxford University Press, 2001)

Morgan, Sally: *Hyenas* (Chrysalis Children's Books, 2003)

Morgan, Sally: *Predators: Lions, Bears, Hyenas* (Chrysalis Children's Books, 2003)

Taylor, Barbara: *Bears* (Chrysalis Children's Books, 2003)

WEBSITES

http://www.nationalgeographic.com/animals
Website of the National Geographic Society, which provides information on thousands of species of animals, as well as conservation news.

http://www.bbc.co.uk/nature/animals/mammals
Website to accompany the *Life of Mammals* television series. Comprehensive site with in-depth articles and behind-the-scenes stories, videos, webcams, interactive challenges and links to other sites.

http://www.abdn.ac.uk/mammal
Website of the Mammal Society (UK), packed with information on British species of mammals with fact sheets, photos, maps, even whale songs. Fun area with quizzes, puzzles and tests, mammal surveys that people can take part in.

Disclaimer
All the Internet addresses (URLs) given in this book were valid at the time of going to press. However, due to the dynamic nature of the Internet, some addresses may have changed, or sites may have changed or ceased to exist since publication. While the author, the packager and Publishers regret any inconvenience this may cause readers, no responsibility for any such changes can be accepted by either the author, the packager or the Publishers.

Index